Mission-shaped Church

John M. Hull is Honorary Professor of Practical Theology in the Queen's Foundation for Ecumenical Theological Education and Emeritus Professor of Religious Education at the University of Birmingham. He is a graduate of the Universities of Melbourne (BA, Bed), Cambridge (MA, LittD) and Birmingham (PhD), and has an honorary DTheol from the University of Frankfurt and an honorary doctorate from the Vrije Universiteit Amsterdam. Brought up in Methodism, he is an Anglican layman and an Elder in the United Reformed Church.

His website is www.johnmhull.biz.

Mission-shaped Church

A Theological Response

John M. Hull

scm press

British Library Cataloguing in Publication data

A catalogue record for this book is available
from the British Library

0 334 04057 4/978 0 334 04057 6

First published in 2006 by SCM Press
9–17 St Albans Place,
London N1 0NX

www.scm-canterburypress.co.uk

SCM Press is a division of
SCM-Canterbury Press Ltd

Printed by Barnwell's Print Ltd
Aylsham, Norfolk NR11 6ET
Tel: 01263 732767

Contents

I would like to express my thanks to the
Allen and Nester Ferguson charitable trust,
whose grant made possible the production of this text.

Introduction

Mission-shaped Church was published by Church House Publishing in 2004. By November 2005 it had sold more than 16,000 copies. The document is the report of a working party set up by the Mission and Public Affairs Council of the Church of England and is commended by the Council for study. Implementation of the recommendations of the report is the responsibility of Fresh Expressions of Church under the leadership of Stephen Croft (www.freshexpressions.org.uk).

The main burden of the report is that the Church of England has depended too much upon the local parish church, and it must now be recognized that this is but one form of church structure. In many ways parish churches are no longer able to meet the needs of the highly mobile society of today. It is necessary to encourage other kinds of ecclesial formation, which may take the form of cell churches, café churches, network associations and so on, and these fresh expressions must be regarded as legitimate churches, genuine churches, although they may lack many features of local parish churches and may indeed sometimes cross parish and even diocesan boundaries. The report is thus a call for the renewal of local church life and a demand for more imaginative structures through which Christian faith can today be expressed. This does not imply that local parish churches will not continue to have an important and perhaps a central place in the life of the church, but the parish church must not be conceived of as the only way that church can be formed. New expressions of church must therefore be encouraged alongside re-vitalized local congregations of the more traditional type.

These recommendations are clearly most timely. Nobody with the interests of the church at heart could fail to approve of the general policy recommended here. It is not surprising that the report has been received with general enthusiasm and that its recommendations are being energetically pursued. My comments are mainly to do with the theological framework of the report, and I do not want my general approval of the practical recommendations of the report to be obscured by my theological reservations. The purpose of my study is to encourage fresh expressions of church by placing them within a theological framework more adequate to the needs of the church and Christian faith today. The fresh expressions of church which are so badly needed deserve better theological support, and may be inhibited if the theological weaknesses of the document are not corrected.

The Church, the Mission and the Kingdom

The theology of the report revolves around certain key concepts: church, mission and kingdom. However, the meaning of these central ideas is not adequately clarified.

> the Church is the fruit of God's mission, and . . . as such it exists to serve and to participate in the ongoing mission of God. (p. xii)

This statement introduces the reader immediately to one of the fundamental theological weaknesses of the report: its failure to distinguish clearly between the church and the mission of God, and consequently its limited ecclesiology and its restricted view of the scope of the Christian mission. The ambiguity in the theology of the report is indicated by the quotation which soon follows in which reference is made to:

> creating new communities of Christian faith as part of the mission of God to express God's kingdom in every geographic and cultural context. (p. xii)

This immediately raises the question as to whether the church is the object of the mission or whether, on the other hand, the church is better regarded as a servant or instrument of the mission. Does the church participate in the mission or is it the outcome of the mission?

From a systematic point of view the report is on solid ground when it declares that 'ecclesiology is a subsection of the doctrine of mission' (p. 24) but this degree of clarity is seldom maintained. Sometimes church, mission and kingdom are simply identified:

> Unless and until the kingdom and the mission are in the DNA of the seed of the church, what is planted will prove to be sterile. If

mission is not located within the identity of church, planting is very unlikely to recover it. (p. 33)

But if ecclesiology is a subset of the doctrine of mission then should we not say that church should be located within the identity of mission? In other words, mission defines church. The church is not the fulfilment or the flowering of mission. The flowering of mission is the Kingdom; church is merely an agent. Therefore, the mission cannot be attained merely by creating churches.

'It is therefore of the essence (the DNA) of the Church to be a missionary community' (p. 85). Although slightly obscured by the botanical metaphor, this statement appears to suggest that the relationship between mission and church is that of essence to existence. The essence is the ideal model, or the potential which, when it comes into actual being, may be described as the existence. But church is not the concrete entity in which mission is actualized. It is undoubtedly true, as the following quotation says, 'There is church because there is mission' (p. 85), but this does not mean that church is the actualization of mission.

Let me clarify this with two illustrations. It is a question of the distinction between purpose or function and the requirement of adequate functioning. The function of a knife is to cut and the requirement of adequate functioning is to be sharp, but it would be wrong to say that the essence of the knife is to be sharp. The essence of an army, its purpose or function, is to fight. Without barracks, uniform and equipment the army cannot function effectively, but that does not mean that the essence of the army is to be found in its barracks, its uniform and its equipment. The purpose or function of mission is to bring in the Kingdom. In order to do this effectively the mission has (among other things) a church. But the mission is not the church.

Sometimes the church is said to be a sign of the Kingdom of God: 'All churches and denominations are called to be signs of the kingdom of God' (p. 34), but the text then distinguishes between being a sign of the Kingdom and being an agent of the Kingdom, referring to Lesslie Newbigin apparently with approval: churches and denominations

> are signs and first fruits but are not to be seen as agents of the Kingdom for that is one role of the Spirit. (p. 34)

The problem is that this way of speaking spiritualizes the Kingdom of God, and removes it from the sphere of history, depriving the church of historical significance. In chapter five, however, an effort is made to have it both ways:

> The church is both the fruit of God's mission – those whom he has redeemed, and the agent of his mission – the community through whom he acts for the world's redemption. (p. 85)

It is significant that even here the church is described as an agent of the mission and not an agent of the Kingdom, and yet one of the goals of the mission is the establishment of the Kingdom.

> What is mission if not the engagement with God in the entire enterprise of bringing the whole of creation to its intended destiny? (p. 85, quoted from Robin Greenwood)

But this is to bring in the Kingdom. Later in the same passage an attempt is made to distinguish the Kingdom of God from the church and from the mission.

> The Son of God expressed this mission in terms of the kingdom of God. The kingdom is a divine activity whereas the Church is a human community. Kingdom agenda and values are often more radical than the church readily allows. In bringing the kingdom, God is on the move and the church is always catching up with him. (p. 86)

But we have been told the church is the product of the triune life of God, as breathed by the Holy Spirit through Christ's sending (p. 85). How then can this distinction between the church as a human institution and the Kingdom as a divine gift be maintained? The correct distinction is between the church as agent and the Kingdom as goal. Moreover, the report continues:

> It is the work of the Spirit to empower the Church to preach and embody that gospel in ways appropriate to each cultural context. (p. 86)

The report agrees that it is:

> the Spirit of Christ by which God, through his church, is drawing all human society to its fulfilment in the Kingdom of God. (p. 86)

Here it would appear to be clear that the church is indeed an agent of the Kingdom of God.

Under the heading 'Jesus, the Church and the Kingdom' a new attempt is made to explain the relationship between these terms:

> The church is a sign and disclosure of the kingdom of God. The kingdom has certain clear qualities – its breaking of social boundaries, its hope for the poor, its message of God's welcome for all, focused in Christ. But it is also presented as something that grows. (p. 94)

This is a reference to the parables of the Kingdom. Since the Kingdom is to grow, then the church, which is a sign of the Kingdom, must also grow. The parables of the Kingdom are regarded as parables of the church. So what has become of the distinction between the Kingdom as a gift and the church as a human institution? The truth is that when it comes to a question of the growth imperative, the Kingdom of God parables are convenient, but when it is a matter of the breaking of social boundaries and the hope of the poor, then the church lags behind the radical character of the Kingdom. Yes, no doubt. But why does not the report call upon the church to manifest the Kingdom of God in exhibiting the signs of the Kingdom as well as through embodying the growth of the Kingdom?

> By virtue of its participation in the life of God, [the church] is not only a sign and instrument, but also a genuine foretaste of God's Kingdom, called to show forth visibly in the midst of history, God's final purposes for humankind. (p. 95, quoted from *Eucharistic Presidency*)

Here the church is certainly very closely associated with the Kingdom.

Does the Confusion Between
Kingdom and Church Matter?

The missiology of *Mission-shaped Church* would have been clearer if it had consistently maintained the view that the church is an instrument or an agent of the mission of God, the outcome of which is to be the Kingdom of God. The mission is sent by God, it is God's sending of God's own being in life for the world. The objective of the mission is the establishment of the Kingdom of God which is the reign of God over all the forces of death, the triumph of love over all the forces of hatred, the triumph of peace over all the forces of violence and warfare. The empirical church is one of the principal agents of this mission; it is one of God's saving projects for the redemption of the world. The church is thus called to participate in the mission of Jesus who proclaimed the coming of the Kingdom in his life, his words and his deeds, and who died and rose again to establish the church as an agent of that Kingdom. The church is a mission project, not the mission itself; the Kingdom of God is the object of the mission, and the life of Jesus Christ continues to be manifest through the church as it witnesses to, embodies and proclaims the Kingdom.

The problem is that the missiology of the report blurs and confuses these distinctions, although the report maintains that the church does not have a mission; rather the mission has a church, at other times the expansion of the church is the mission. The church is to be a sign and an expression, even an agent of the Kingdom when it is a question of the inevitable and pre-destined growth of the church, but when it is a question of the church exhibiting good news for the poor and the breaking down of social boundaries in the interests of justice, then the church is only a human institution which cannot be expected to do anything but lag behind the Kingdom. But does this confusion matter? I shall argue that it matters very much indeed, and for the following reasons.

It is in chapter five 'Theology for a Missionary Church' that the implications of the conceptual ambiguities I have described emerge clearly:

> the Church is God's community with a divine mandate to repro-
> duce. It is intended by God to multiply, by the Spirit, and to fill
> all creation. This is an essential dimension of any missionary
> ecclesiology. Churches are created by God to grow. (p. 93)

This does not necessarily apply to every local church but 'we do argue that it is the normative condition for the national church in normal times if it keeps the faith and keeps up with the culture' (p. 93, quoted from Bob Jackson). This mandate is based in the creation by God of the human race 'with a mandate to govern the earth with justice. From its inception God's human community was to reproduce itself biologically, in order to fulfil the divine purpose' (p. 93). In the New Testament Jesus is described as the second Adam, and 'the church is intended to be a new humanity'. It is 'to reproduce itself through mission, and so to fill the earth' (p. 93). Not only is the creation of human beings seen as a justification for the domination of the church but the calling of Abraham is regarded as providing additional support. The family of Abraham was to become as numerous as the stars of the heaven, not for its own sake but for the benefit of all the families on earth. The followers of Jesus are the true children of Abraham in fulfilment of the Genesis and Abrahamic promises. Thus through its inheritance of the covenants between God and Adam, and between God and Abraham, the church is destined to fill the earth. 'The story of the young church, and the dynamics by which it came to birth, bear witness to a Church born to reproduce' (p. 95). The 'ultimate destiny of the church' implies that 'growth, by reproduction, will be vital to fill the earth' (p. 95).

Now if I, as someone sympathetic to Islam but not a Muslim, were to read such words in a document written with authority by senior leaders of Islam and commended by a responsible, representative association of Muslims, I would be thoroughly alarmed. I would regard it as the announcement of an imperialism which acknowledges no diversity, tolerates no rivals and is bent upon world domination. I would not be surprised if a Muslim reading *Mission-shaped Church* was alarmed in the same way and for similar reasons. What? Fill the earth? But if the church is to fill the earth there will be no standing room for Jews or Muslims, Buddhists or Hindus. All these, together with any remaining humanists or atheists, are to be crowded out. There is no recognition of the fact that Jews and Muslims also regard themselves as children of Abraham. This is the result of a theology which regards the church as the fruit of the mission of God, and identifies the church with the Kingdom of God.

Which church are we speaking about? It is the national church. Which national church? 'The intention here is not primarily to provide a blanket theological underpinning for all new forms of church, but to suggest some theological principles that should influence all decisions about the shape of the Church of England at this time of missionary opportunity' (p. 84).

The report is quite specific that the mission about which it speaks is that of the Church of England, which exists 'to be a church for the nation'. The text continues:

> this is not a comment on the issue of the church being established, but a statement of its mission purpose. (p. 35)

But if we leave the establishment of the Church of England on one side, if we propose to ignore it and simply to speak about the mission of the church, the question inevitably arises as to why the Church of England should be a church for the nation – that is, have a mission for the nation – any more than any other denomination. Is the Church in Wales to be a church for all people in Wales? Would not other Welsh churches be entitled, if any church is entitled, to make similar claims? And if we leave out its establishment, why should the Church in England (the expression is used on p. 39) be any different?

> The Anglican calling, because of theological conviction, is to be a church for all. (p. 35)

This comment immediately follows the discussion of the parish system and the increasing gaps in that system and thus flows from the broken territorialism of the Church of England. It is meant to be a church for all because the parochial system covered the entire country, but if we are talking about mission rather than territorial, geographical coverage, the Methodists have just as much claim to be a church for all.

> Church planting and fresh expressions of church can help to identify and begin to fill the geographical and cultural gaps. (p. 35)

That is, to resume the territorial privilege.

> To be a Church for the nation, the holes in our national network need to be filled. To be Anglican is to want to be rooted in communities and to be accessible to those communities (however those communities define themselves). (p. 35)

This argument indicates the struggle of the national church to be and remain a land church, a struggle to reject the congregational model of the church as a people who are called out locally in favour of a church which has a theological mandate to be everywhere and for all.

> Anglican history is the outworking of the Church's belief that this country is its mission field and pastoral responsibility. (p. 36)

Church is a 'community with a divine mandate to reproduce' (p. 93). So the situation is not just that the church intends to fill the whole earth and to offer no place to other faiths and commitments, but within England the Church of England claims the right to occupy all of England, and this not so much because of its established character but because of its characteristically Anglican theology of mission. There appears to be no standing room for Methodists, United Reformed Church or Roman Catholics. The latter, by implication, must be considered intruders into the divinely given territorial mission of the Church of England. Is not this theology of Anglicanism not only unrealistic but preposterous? When we read in the opening paragraphs of chapter seven that provisions must be made for non-territorial and network churches, it is hard to believe that in order to be consistent with the Anglican theology of this report, these can be anything other than steps toward repossession of the territory, notwithstanding the protestation 'We are not about patching the fabric of that old garment' (p. 126). When considering structures,

> Decisions also need to be made in the light of conversations with other denominations, so that what is proposed connects well and respects the mission initiatives and intentions of those other denominations. (p. 139)

And one can learn from other denominations (p. 143). This is generous, but it would have rung more true if when discussing the role of the Bishop in chapter seven, there had been some endorsement of the missionary theology and mandate of the non-Episcopal churches.

The Problem of Diversity

Diversity is a recurrent theme throughout the report. In his foreword, the Archbishop of Canterbury Dr Rowan Williams says:

> There is plenty of theological room for diversity . . . This immediately raises large questions about how different churches can keep in contact and learn from each other. (p. vii)

Williams is speaking of the variety of local church structures which will supplement the traditional parish model. This variety

> is a pattern that looks ahead to the diversity, brought from all corners of the earth, that will be celebrated in God's eschatological reality. (p. 13)

The distinction between networks and territory, increasingly common in the church planting movement since the 1990s, has created such a variety of patterns of church that it can be called 'an explosion of diversity' (p. 20) and as the years have gone by there has been a growing diversification in types of church plantings. This is grounded in the Holy Trinity,

> which models diversity as well as unity. Creation reveals God's affirmation of diversity. Mission to a diverse world legitimately requires a diverse Church. Catholicity should not be interpreted as monochrome oneness. Election and incarnation reveal God daring to be culturally specific within diverse contexts. (p. 20)

This means that the new church structures must not seek merely to duplicate existing church structures:

the label 'Church Growth' can suggest church planting is about adding to the number of existing churches, whereas at best it is about multiplying diverse future churches. (p. 23)

It is clear that in *Mission-shaped Church* the concept of diversity does not go beyond the call for more diverse patterns of church. Too often, it is said, the church plants of ten years ago were regarded as bridges into traditional churches (p. 23) but now more diverse kinds of church must be acknowledged as having integrity in themselves and not as being merely introductions or recruiting points for a kind of traditional normality. Diversity, as the report sees it, is a new and challenging stage in the concept of church planting. Although it is claimed that this is a response to the diversity of creation, there is little or no recognition of wider diversity. Wherever there is an occasion to deal with the wider diversity of religions, values and lifestyles, these are treated negatively. We are witnessing the

> death of the culture that formerly conferred Christian identity upon the British people as a whole . . . The Christian story is no longer at the heart of the nation . . . Our multicultural and multi-faith society reinforces a consumerist view that faiths and their differences are simply issues of personal choice, to be decided on the basis of what 'works' and what makes you happy. (p. 11)

There is here no acknowledgement of the enrichment of British society through the presence of other ethnicities and religious groups but only an admission that Christian values have been undermined. 'The reality is that mainstream culture no longer brings people to the church door' (p. 11). The emergence of the multicultural and consumerist society is an issue which should provoke Christian repentance. 'We have allowed our culture and the Church to drift apart' (p. 13).

The next reference to the plurality of British society comes in the context of a discussion about the problem of a specific denomination, such as the Church of England is widely perceived to be, winning the allegiance of contemporary Christians. Many modern Christians are non-denominational in their outlook.

> Surrounded by secularism, materialism, competing spiritual movements and other world religions, simply being authentic Christians

seems sufficient to them . . . denominations per se are not seen as desirable designer labels, only as different types of clothing, most of which are not thought 'cool'. (p. 25)

Local ecumenical partnerships are not thought to be very effective replies to this situation. Diversity, in other words, is problematic because it undermines denominational plausibility.

Confirmation of this negative attitude toward religious and cultural diversity in Britain is found in the diagram setting out the religious affiliations and practices of people in England (p. 37). This

> is not attempting to take account of the church involvement . . . of people who are members of other world faiths and traditions (6 per cent of the population in the 2001 census). (p. 36)

Among those who have left church and who are now closed to the possibility of returning to church, one of the reasons given was 'other world religions' (p. 38). At first glance, a more positive approach toward cultural diversity is indicated in the material which follows the heading 'Christ and Culture'. The relationship of the gospel to culture is always expressed in diversity. Justin Martyr taught that the Logos *spermatikos*, the seed-bearing word, was made visible in Christ but was also present in the Greek world before Christ. Justin thought that there were truths of philosophy which might be attributed to the workings of the same Logos (p. 86). However, the conclusion which the report draws from this is much less radical:

> Hence, conversion ought not to involve the transfer of individuals from their native culture to the culture of the church, so much as the conversion of their culture enriching the cultural life of the church. (p. 87)

Yes, but what has happened to the recognition of the work of the Logos in other cultures? In the Kingdom of God,

> justice comes for the poor, peace to the nations and all visions of race, culture and national identity disappear as we discover we are all family together and we worship our God for ever. (p. 89)

The Spirit makes it possible to experience something of this kingdom unity within the present diverse body of the Church. (pp. 89–90)

Yes, but not, as Justin Martyr and Clement of Alexandria believed, beyond the church.

There is one more reference to other religions. Various types of church growth are discussed, including 'bridging growth'. This refers to planting at a distance from the mother church or in a

distanced culture, such as among a different language group, or for adherents of another world religion. (p. 107)

Presumably the report has in mind some kind of proselytizing activity but this remains unstated. One wonders if this is what is intended when it is recommended that 'cross-cultural training should be an inherent part of ministerial theological education' (p. 108).

A new perspective is found on the question of diversity by the discussion of the 'Homogeneous Unit Principle' advocated by the American conservative missiologist, Donald McGavran:

'People like to become Christian without crossing racial/linguistic/class/cultural barriers.' In other words, they prefer to remain who they are culturally while changing to being Christian. Culturally they remain the same and tend to gather with others from the same culture who share their faith. (p. 108)

McGavran based his policy upon his missionary experience in India, where church plants were most successful if class and caste barriers were not challenged. In summarizing responses to the McGavran principle of homogeneity, the report mentions the fact that there are those Christians who believe that followers of Jesus Christ should seek to break down barriers. But one reply, the report suggests, to this is to affirm

the diversity of creation. God is Creator of all, and is also Creator of specific and diverse cultures. Whilst elements of all cultures are damaged by the Fall, like the rest of creation, culture is part of God's handiwork. (p. 108)

This, however, is to use the concept of diversity to argue for the separate development of races and cultures. It is the basic principle of apartheid.

A second argument is now provided in favour of McGavran's principle of homogeneity. This is drawn, surprisingly enough, from the doctrine of the incarnation of Jesus Christ. The church planter should follow the example of Jesus in choosing a specific culture and time into which to be born:

> The incarnation principle points to the planting of churches that are culture-specific for those being reached. (p. 108)

No reference is made to the creation of a community of inclusive love by Jesus, and the report seems unaware that its theology of apartheid makes nonsense of the ideal of the inclusive church, which is referred to elsewhere in its pages.

On page 109 a third reason to support McGavran is suggested. Use is now made of the radical concept of God's preferential option for the poor to support the idea of monochrome churches.

A third factor comes from the theology of Good News for the Oppressed. Sociological study shows that when two cultures are together in a social context, a healthy, heterogeneous culture does not result – one tends to dominate the other. The culture of those with the educational and economic power tends to come out on top. An attempt at diversity becomes dominance (p. 109).

Good news for the poor, the argument continues,

> is only truly good news when it empowers the poor or marginalised to form their own communities of faith, in which indigenous people work together for change and renewal. (p. 109)

This is certainly a novel interpretation of God's preferential option for the poor, a subject that has not received much attention earlier in the report. So the poor are to be kept separated from the educated so that the educated will not dominate them. I would like to know if this is indeed the policy being recommended to the Church of England. Can it be good news to the poor to encourage them to stay in poverty? The complacency toward the economically powerful indicated by this part of the report is quite breathtaking. What has become of the brave words about the church dying to be reborn amidst another culture? The marginalized are to be encouraged to form their own churches rather than struggling to overcome their marginalization! The misuse of one of the most prophetic insights of contemporary theology, the preferential option of God for the poor, is almost cynical in its nonchalance.

Might it be defended on the grounds that this and other arguments in favour of the homogeneity principle are supposed to be merely descriptive, and not to be read as the views of the report itself? This seems unlikely. The possible reasons for the policy are presented with apparent sympathy. There is no note of dissent or reserve.

It is not even clear that the authors of the report have correctly understood what Donald McGavran means by the 'homogeneity principle'. His preferred expression is 'people movement', by which McGavran means that in many primal societies, conversion is to take place on the part of a whole people rather than isolated individuals extracted from their native community. In the Christianized countries of the West, however, individuals would not usually have to renounce their local community when becoming Christian, and therefore the concept of a people movement is impossible in principle in a largely Christian country. On the contrary, the questions of racial, social and political justice are the fully justified concerns of churches in the West (McGavran, 1955, p. 15). (There is thus no reason to think that Donald McGavran would have approved of a mission policy in England which ignored or even perpetuated the divisions between rich and poor; he would on the contrary have considered the overcoming of such distinctions an important part of what he called the 'perfecting' of the church in a society where poverty was already regarded as unacceptable, and would have encouraged churches to seek for the conversion of individuals and not the creation of homogeneous movements.)

Having thus, in its own way, reviewed the arguments for and

against what it takes to be Donald McGavran's policy of creating homogeneous Christian communities, the report does not commit itself, but blandly suggests that

> the answer may be to accept initial cultural similarity while seeking gradual cultural diversity, expressed in interdependence between groups unlike one another. (p. 109)

It seems that the groups are to remain separate but interdependent. There could be little doubt, however, who will be dependent upon whom.

In short, while encouraging diversity within the church, the report shows little interest in difference outside the church, and little awareness of the church as engaged in resistance to racial and economic differences. The hope is that ultimately all human diversity will be gathered into the single church which will fill the earth.

Christendom

Mission-shaped Church regards the situation of the church as being in 'post Christendom', referring to:

> the death of the culture that formerly conferred Christian identity upon the British people as a whole. (p. 11)

This situation has been brought on by the plurality and the possible relativity of religions and life stances. The report observes that:

> The consequences for a national church, used to operating among people and institutions on the assumptions of Christendom, are acute. (p. 11)

It is this post-Christendom situation in which

> Very many people have no residue of Christian faith at all; it's not just dormant, it's non-existent. (p. 12, quoted from *Church Army News*)

The nature of Christendom is returned to in chapter five: 'We have put emphasis upon the demise of Christendom' (p. 84). The problem is: what is a land church to do when Christendom is no more?

> Despite the substantial work done on 'Gospel and Culture' in recent years, the Church of England has not yet drawn significantly upon the world Church's experience in cross-cultural mission . . . This is due, in part, to assumptions about Christendom, blinding our imaginations about the form of the Church. (p. 90)

The question, however, which must be asked is whether the report, in realizing that the response of the Church of England has been vitiated by nostalgia for Christendom, succeeds in breaking away from that fascination.

That question may be answered if we study chapter one of the report. The purpose of the chapter is to 'explore how we are called to be and to do church':

> the Church of England aims to be a Church for everyone in the country, being truly among them as Jesus was with the people of his day. (p. 1)

For this reason it is necessary to examine the culture of England 'so we can see the possible shape, or shapes, of church to which God is calling us' (p. 1). A number of statistical trends are then discussed. These deal with increased mobility, the changing patterns of family life, particularly during weekends and similar matters, and the conclusion is that 'This will inevitably make Sunday church attendance problematic' (p. 3). Typical of the concern that lies behind the selection of statistics is the sentence:

> The rise in the number of single people, and the delay in having children, means that there is a significant group of people in their twenties who do not have children, so child-friendly activities (and, indeed, morning activities at the weekend) may not be something they can relate to. (p. 4)

There follows a review of weekend behaviour, concluding with the comment: 'People no longer view Sunday as special or as "church time"' (p. 4). 'Children are much more likely to be playing sport than being in Sunday school or church' (p. 4). The character of neighbourhood is changing and giving way to a whole series of networks. This leads to the conclusion that

> The planting of churches among the mobile and among the poor is integral to the Church of England's mission. (pp. 6f)

Only some such policy will:

adequately fulfil the incarnational principle and demons
universality of Christ's Lordship in all expressions of
(p. 8)

These first eight pages of the report set the theme for what follows. No interest is shown in the study of British society for its own sake but only in so far as it creates a problem for the typical Sunday worship of the parish church. What is offered instead is an entirely church-centred view of social change, yet it is described as the incarnational principle. Christendom refers to that period in the history of Europe when there was an unbroken integrity of land, people and faith. Such an approach to British society is no longer possible or permissible. How can the Church of England or any Christian church be a church for all the people in England, when millions of them belong to other religions? Once again we see this indifference to the positive features of plurality, this failure to acknowledge diversity, which is a feature of the Christendom approach.

The next few pages seem to be more interesting. British society is now discussed as a culture of consumption. Instead of discovering identity through what we produce, we find it through what we consume: 'We are what we buy' (p. 9). At the heart of such a culture lies choice. Religion is less likely to be a matter of traditional culture and more likely to be regarded as a matter of choice.

This is both interesting and insightful, but what use is made of it in the unfolding logic of *Mission-shaped Church*? The attitude of the report toward the consuming society is one of acquiescence:

In one sense there is no alternative to a consumer society. That is what we are, that is where we are and that is where we must be church and embody the gospel. (p. 10)

There is no trace here of Ulrich Duchrow's (1995) alternatives to global capitalism! Instead of leading to a prophetic role for the church, the report concludes that the church needs to adapt itself to the culture of choice by providing more varieties of expressions of church. The same sense of inevitability is found in the comment:

> Although Western culture will continue to evolve (particularly through technological change) it has taken a shape that it is likely to hold for the foreseeable future. (p. 13)

The discussion concludes:

> The demise of Christendom reduces radically the temptations of power, clearing space for the old story to be retold. (p. 13)

It would not be unfair, however, to comment that having bewailed the demise of Christendom, the report then goes on to suggest ways of re-establishing it.

A Deuteronomic Spirituality

The working party believes that the situation they describe is, to a significant degree, the fault of the churches themselves:

> This is also a moment for repentance. We have allowed our culture and the Church to drift apart, without our noticing. We need the grace of the Spirit for repentance if we are to receive a fresh baptism of the Spirit for witness. (p. 13)

> If the decline of the Church is ultimately caused neither by the irrelevance of Jesus, nor by the indifference of the community, but by the Church's failure to respond fast enough to an evolving culture, to a changing spiritual climate, and to the promptings of the Holy Spirit, then that decline can be addressed by the repentance of the Church. . . . A diocese or parish, which, out of repentance, grows a new relevance to the contemporary world, may also grow in numbers and strength because the Spirit of Jesus has been released to do his work. (p. 14)

The church, for most people, the report continues,

> is either an utterly foreign culture, or one that they have decided to reject. For the Church in England, the stark reality of this situation should be a cause for profound repentance and renewed missionary endeavour. (p. 39)

Indeed, keeping the faith is a condition for the growth of the national church. Churches are created by God to grow. This does not necessarily apply to every local church, but 'we do argue that it is the normative condition for the national church in normal times, if it keeps the faith and keeps up with the culture' (p. 93). I take this to mean that the authors of the report believe that there should be overall growth. There seems to be no particular reason why the national church, i.e. the Church of England, should be singled out as destined to grow any more than, say, the Baptist Union or the Salvation Army, but the point the report is making in its curiously national way is that while individual local congregations may not grow, the denomination as a whole should normally be in a condition of growth. The significant point, however, for my present purposes, is to note that if this growth is not taking place, it is because the church has not kept faith or has not kept up with the culture. In other words, if there is no growth, it is the church's own fault.

Timothy Gorringe (1994) has described as the modern Deuteronomists those Christians who are attached to the Deuteronomic cycle. First the nation prospers, then sin enters in and the nation is punished. The punishment takes the form of a period of oppression or disaster, at which the nation repents. God hears the cry of repentance, and brings salvation. So the nation prospers, and the cycle can begin all over again.

I am critical of the use of the Deuteronomic cycle as found in *Mission-shapedChurch* for several reasons. First, in attaching blame to church members for the failure of the church to grow, the report does not take seriously enough the secularization process the significance of the regional factor – Christian faith seems to be growing in every continent except Europe. It ignores the history through which the British churches have passed, during which time the pressures of modernity and now the pluralism of postmodernity have created a very different climate from that of Christendom in the late middle ages. The use of the Deuteronomic cycle as an explanation for the situation of the churches seems to suggest that thinking Christians need take no notice of the contributions of the social and historical sciences in seeking an understanding of the situation of religion today.

My second reason for feeling uncomfortable with this use of the Deuteronomic cycle is that not only does its use obscure the very significant trends outside the church which are impacting upon faith but because it directs the attention of individual Christians and churches toward their inner life, and sets up barriers which are likely to prevent a serious examination of other factors. This may, indeed, be a partial explanation for the superficiality of the social, cultural and economic analysis in the report itself.

Finally, the Deuteronomic cycle is clearly unhelpful as a pastoral policy. Its application is likely to result in feelings of guilt; indeed, it is apparently intended to arouse such feelings. It sets up a culture of internal blame, and is thus not a positive contribution to Christian renewal.

Inculturation

Inculturation theory is a significant aspect of contemporary missiology (Donovan, 1982; Scherer and Bevans, 1999). The older concept was indigenization, but it was increasingly seen that this implied that there was a normal, natural home culture of Christian faith and this could be distinguished from the other, foreign cultures into which Christianity had to be planted. Indigenization suggested the model of sending churches and receiving churches. The alternative 'adaptation' was discussed but the growth of inter-cultural studies and the contributions to missiology made by interpretative anthropology encouraged use of the expression 'inculturation'. 'Contextualization' is also used, and although the lineage of this expression is different, its meaning is rather similar.

The report acknowledges that the Church of England has, on the whole, been fairly resistant toward the inculturation debate:

> Despite the substantial work done on 'Gospel and culture' in recent years, the Church of England has not yet drawn significantly upon the world Church's experience in cross-cultural mission. (p. 90)

With a flash of real insight the report continues by remarking that this resistance may be due to the persistence in the Church of England of the assumptions of Christendom. How then does the report envisage the inculturation of Christian faith within England?

> No serious attempt at inculturation by the Church of England can begin with a fixed view of the outward form of the local church. (p. 91)

It is not clear to me why this should be restricted to the local church while the national church apparently remains exempt from this process. The authors of the report are very clear about the need to both inculturate the church within the consuming culture and to create within it a counter-culture:

> The everyday challenge of consumerism is yet to be fully acknow-ledged by most Christian communities. (p. 91, quoted from David Lyon)

This is an encouraging remark, but unfortunately it is not followed through. It becomes simply a question of creating network churches, because the culture is tending in that direction, of creating café churches since cafés are popular, and so on. Since choice is the central feature of consumerism, Christians should think in terms other than parish structure, and in that way, choice will in a sense be counter-cultural. Instead of contributing to consumerism, it will display the Lordship of Christ. This is certainly an ingenious argument for encouraging church members to get off the pews of their parish churches, but is it a sufficiently radical attack upon the consumer culture?

The favourite model for the inculturation process used in the report is that of the incarnation:

> It is the incarnation of the gospel, within a dominantly consumer society, that provides the Church of England with its major mis-sionary challenge. (p. xiii)

The creation of patterns of both neighbourhood and parish churches 'will adequately fulfil the incarnational principle' (p. 8).

> Election and incarnation reveal God daring to be culturally specific within diverse contexts. (p. 20)

A clue to the implementation within British culture lies in the kenotic Christology whereby Christ emptied himself to enter into his culture. So the parish churches must be ready to become immanent within various forms of cultural life (p. 89).

It is difficult to feel altogether at ease with the way the doctrine of the incarnation is used and interpreted here. For example, one of the kinds of new church structures is compared with a seed that is blown on the wind, perhaps a long way from its originating plant, and may make a new beginning where this type of plant was previously unknown:

> People on seed teams move their home in order to plant, so that they can identify more deeply with the area to which they are called. (p. 115)

This type of church best illustrates the missionary dynamic of dying to their previous identity in order to re-incarnate the Gospel and the church in the missionary context. Jesus Christ is here compared to a transplant from another world, a seed blown from afar, something alien coming into a strange place. This kind of high Alexandrine Christology is not at all at home in the contemporary debate about the inculturation of the gospel. This is because in the report, two features of inculturation are noticeably missing. The first is the thought that the Gospel is already present in the receiving culture prior to the arrival of explicit Christian faith. There must be places in the local culture with which Christian faith has some kind of affinity. One of the tasks of mission is to identify those points of contact. Jesus Christ did not enter an alien world: 'He came to that which was his own, but his own did not receive him' (John 1.11). There is no trace in *Mission-shaped Church* of the methodology of seeking in the surrounding culture for rumours of angels or signals of transcendence.

Second, in the inculturation discussion it is not just the mission that is inculturated but the gospel itself. The report certainly deals with the implantation of mission but not with the inculturation of theology. The nature of Christian faith is not problematic in this report. The inculturation debate is interesting and radical because it raises the question about the universality of Christian faith. If faith is to be inculturated within very different cultures, how does one distinguish the constants (if there are any) which make it possible to identify Christian faith from one culture to another? There is no trace of this discussion in the report. It would not be going too far to say that the report makes use of the concept of inculturation to justify and promote the idea of diverse forms of church, but although it speaks a great deal of the sacrificial death involved in this adaptation, the sacrifice involved is always merely structural, never conceptual, never theological, never a matter of the nature of faith itself. The external, almost impersonal character of the understanding of mission in the report is seen rather clearly in what is intended to be no more than a passing comment. The very nature of the church is mission:

> There is church because there is mission, not vice versa. Apart from worship, everything else is secondary to this. (p. 85)

But why make an exception of worship? If church is mission and if worship is the heart of church, then worship is also mission. The church does not mission for the sake of worship; it worships for the sake of mission. If someone were to reply that worship is surely for the sake of God alone, I point out that the mission is the mission of God. This is one of the fundamental distinctions between the church militant and the church triumphant. The church triumphant, the church in heaven, can worship God free from any other consideration. But for the church militant, the church on earth, everything must be subordinate to mission. The church, as the report insists, is the body of Christ, the continuation of the incarnation of Christ, and worship does not represent a transcendental area immune from the concrete character of incarnation. In the life of the church militant, if worship becomes an end in itself, immune from the missionary nature of the church, it becomes a fetish. Worship is instrumental to mission. Worship provides resources and motivation for mission by recalling Christians into the presence of the God who sends. It was in worship that Isaiah heard the Lord crying, 'Whom shall I send? And who will go for us?' (Isaiah 6.8).

The Prophetic Church

I began this discussion of *Mission-shaped Church* by pointing out that concepts such as Kingdom and church, gospel and mission were not distinguished clearly, consistently or acceptably. I now want to return to the concept of mission itself. When we wish to speak of the purpose of Christian faith in history, we refer to Christian mission. Missiology is the critical, historical and theological study of the purpose of God in history as understood by Christian faith. Missiology as a branch of theology has attracted huge interest in the past 50 years or so (Bosch, 1991). The reasons for this are worth mentioning. Historical scholarship has shown that Christian self-understanding of Christian purpose in history has varied considerably over the centuries. This has problematized the concept of mission, since if it has varied over the centuries it will presumably continue to vary. This means that the nature of mission can no longer be taken for granted, as if it were naturally given in the very structure of Christian faith, but the factors leading to the variations in understanding of mission must be understood, and the mission must be deliberately and responsibly reinterpreted.

A second reason for the problematization of mission in recent decades has been the evident failure to convert the world to Christian faith, an intention and a hope which was held firmly in the nineteenth century at least. The rise of modern secular movements such as humanism and communism, growing contact and dialogue between world faiths, the cultural shift at least in the West from enlightenment to postmodernity and the phenomenon of contemporary globalization are among the factors that have demanded a reconsideration of the meaning and purpose of Christian faith today. Thoughtful Christians often find it quite difficult to consider what Christian faith is for, in the global and historical sense. This difficulty persists in spite of the fact that devotionally, intellectually and experientially one may continue to find personal commitment to Christian faith enriching and satisfying. Nevertheless, there is or ought to be some compatibility between the subjectivity of the Christian individual and his or her understanding of the broad destiny of Christian faith, unless the individual is willing to live an unreflective life, simply enjoying the private satisfactions of faith. It is clear then that reflecting on Christian mission necessarily involves reflection upon the nature of Christian faith itself, and this in turn must influence one's subjective appropriation of faith.

Elsewhere (Hull, 1999) I have discussed the distinctions suggested by Raimundo Panikkar between Christendom, Christianity and Christian-ness. Panikkar suggests that Christendom was the period when Christian faith in Europe possessed an integrity of territory, culture and faith. This period may be thought of as having begun with the Christianization of the Roman Empire and as continuing until the European Renaissance. Christianity refers to the Christian belief system as a structure comparable to and in competition with other somewhat similar belief structures. This concept emerged in the seventeenth century as a result of reflection upon the implications of the European voyages of discovery, the encounters between Christian faith and the religions of Asia and the primal world, and may to some extent be regarded as a projection on the intellectual level of the political and economic competition between the European empires and the world they were seeking to dominate. They sought to fill the earth, and Christianity was their vehicle. The period of Christianity in that sense is now coming to an end. The concept of Christianity understood in this way is now seen to be lacking in innocence, and the competition between world religions is now seen to be redolent of an ideological past which must now be surpassed by a period of partnership and mutuality. If this is rejected, the only way forward for Christian faith would seem to be into a more hardened and shrewdly competitive attempt at Christian world dominance.

'Christian-ness' may be a useful word to describe the revival of discipleship to Jesus Christ which alone can provide an effective rationale for living Christian life today. These three concepts – Christendom, Christianity and Christian-ness – may provide useful distinctions when reflecting upon Christian mission. In light of this, *Mission-shaped Church* is a somewhat curious document. It is highly conscious of the rise of Christendom, barely mentions Christianity, and is surprisingly free from any trace of what might broadly be called Christian-ness – not that one would expect to find this particular word, but Christian faith as suggested by the word 'Christian-ness' is almost completely lacking in the report. The term 'Christianity' refers to this faith among others, and since the report does not acknowledge the diversity of faiths, there is no reason to mention Christianity.

During the period of Christendom the fundamental biblical verse which was thought of as authorizing Christian mission was 'compel them to come in' (Luke 14.23). Since there could be no plurality within Christendom, deviant groups within and newly discovered people beyond Christendom must be compelled to enter. During the period of Christianity the Christian mission found its authority in what came to be known in the nineteenth century as the Great Commission. This is found in Matthew 28 where the resurrected Jesus commands his followers to go into all the world making disciples of all the nations and baptizing them in the name of the Father, the Son and the Holy Spirit. Although these verses have not lost their charismatic power, for many today Christian mission is better expressed in the self-under-standing of Jesus as reported by Luke in the Nazareth sermon: 'The Spirit of the Lord is upon me, because he has anointed me to bring good news to the poor. He has sent me to proclaim freedom for the prisoners' (Luke 4.18).

This insight was memorably expressed by the Willingen conference of 1952, where the theology of the *missio dei* became prominent. It has become a central theme of missiology since then (Philip, 1999). Christian mission is not a mission of the church; but church itself is a feature of mission. The mission is God's mission. God as Father, Son and Spirit turned toward the world that God has made in mercy and compassion, the world in which God has created life. This mission, expressed most powerfully in the commitment of God in Christ to the point of death and beyond death is expressed through the church as well as through everything that God as creator, God as reconciler and God as life-giver is for the world. The effect of this revolutionary thinking was to readjust the relationship between church and mission.

All of this is expressed very well in *Mission-shaped Church* which, nevertheless, strangely misses the point. In spite of its best intentions, and contrary to its professed theology, *Mission-shaped Church* continues to view mission through the lens of the church instead of viewing the church through the lens of mission; in *Mission-shaped Church* Christian faith is viewed through the eyes of the church rather than allowing the church to be viewed through the eyes of Christian faith.

In order to illustrate this, let us examine what *Mission-shaped Church* says about poverty. The report is aware of the patterns of exclusion and inclusion created by the 'technological rich and technological poor' (p. 5) in the communications world and that this is driven by financial interests. Moreover, the

> planting of churches among the mobile and among the poor is integral to the Church of England's mission. (pp. 6f)

This is further emphasized as follows:

> The scriptural command 'that we remember the poor' is given to all Christians, and so it is incumbent on all churches exploring church planting or fresh expressions of church to consider God's call to the poor. (p. 7)

In its analysis of the consumer society, the report emphasizes the exclusion of the poor. 'The poor are those who cannot buy things. A consumer society excludes the poor. For the first time in history, the poor are un-functional and useless' (p. 10). At this point, *Mission-shaped Church*, in perceiving the break between labour and capital, hovers on the edge of a genuine prophetic insight, but this receives no further development. This may partly be a reflection of reluctant acquiescence in the capitalist society of consumption which is adopted here as discussed above, but the main reason is probably the fact that the interests of the working party were not focused upon poverty but upon the church.

In chapter four, where fresh expressions of church are reviewed, there is an interesting discussion about the Basic Ecclesial Communities (BECS), which originated in Latin America. They:

offer a gospel of liberation: a church of the poor for the poor . . .
They seek to bring hope and challenge – hope to the oppressed,
and challenge that together people can work for a better society.
(p. 47)

The report says that these small Christian communities are widely
respected because:

they seek to hold together agendas for radical change with commitment to historic order. (p. 48)

However, the report continues,

their commitment to radical justice and the priority of the local has
led to some nervous central reactions. (p. 48)

It is not made clear whether the report considers these nervous central
reactions justified or not. The problem was that it was difficult to find
examples of Anglican BECs. This may be, as the report indicates,
because:

much English leadership training demands an enculturation into
middle class values, which is either alien to, or serves to alienate,
leaders from UPA society. (p. 49)

However, the report makes no comment upon the implications of this
situation. Describing the outcome of the Christian mission, we read:

It is a future in which justice comes for the poor, peace to the nations
and all visions of race, culture and national identity disappear as
we discover we are all family together and we worship our God for
ever. (p. 89)

It is recognized that:

The Kingdom has certain clear qualities – its breaking of social
boundaries, its hope for the poor, its message of God's welcome for
all. (p. 94)

Not until chapter six, however, does the problem of poverty become a topic for discussion. This arises in connection with Donald McGavran and the policy of creating homogeneous Christian communities, to which I drew attention above in a different connection. In one of the most daring and original parts of the report, the 'theology of Good News for the Oppressed' becomes an argument for keeping congregations of rich and poor people separate:

> the Church of England's broad failure to express church within the culture of the urban poor is the chief reason why the Anglican church has seldom effectively reached them. Good news for the poor is only truly good news when it empowers the poor or marginalized to form their own communities of faith. (p. 109)

This is a grave error. The poor are empowered not by having their own poor churches but by escaping from poverty. The complacency and insensitivity of *Mission-shaped Church* at this point is truly incredible.

Conclusions

> Start with the Church and the mission will probably get lost. Start
> with mission and it is likely that the Church will be found. (p. 124)

This is a fine sentence. It is one of the many insights which are found
in *Mission-shaped Church*. Nevertheless, the implications of these
insights are seldom followed through.

It is regrettable that the working party did not adopt a different
approach to its task. The problem they wished to deal with is that the
local parish church often seems to be stuck in a cycle of decline. This
has been discussed in a number of balanced, thoughtful and theo-
logically responsible studies, such as those by Steven Croft (2002)
and Robert Warren (2004). However, instead of seeking to gather up
the observations and suggestions made by such authors, the working party placed its study in the tradition of the church growth and
church planting movements, and particularly the 1994 report on
church planting. Indeed, *Mission-shaped Church* thinks of itself as
a ten-year follow-up of this document. It would have been better if
the work had been thought of as a 40-year follow-up of the famous
report *The Missionary Structure of the Congregation* (World Council
of Churches, 1964). This makes rather similar suggestions about local
variety but sets it in a more satisfactory theological vision.

It was certainly necessary to give solid support to the movements
to create new expressions of church, and to give a lead to those wor-
ried about the problem of parish boundaries, ecclesial authority and
that kind of thing. But this could have been done in a report simply
entitled *Varieties of Local Church*, or indeed *Fresh Expressions of
Church*. The lineage of church planting encouraged the working party
to become excessively church centred in their theology, and their sense

of urgency, added to the desire to encourage and motivate local congregations, led them into a missiology too expansive for the task. They set out to offer a theology of growth, but mere expansion of parish churches would not have met the bill, and so it was necessary to distinguish between growth through cloning and growth through bi-sexual reproduction; and the working party found itself embroiled in a slightly absurd series of metaphors. The report presents us with this vision of the whole creation moving on towards the freedom of the children of God, so to speak, and then produces nothing more than a demand for more café churches. Problems about Anglican identity further confused the issue, and led to further grandiose speculations. Unlike the United Reformed Church, the Church of England does not have local churches because of a theology of locality but for historical reasons going back into the pre-Reformation period. So all that is necessary to encourage different kinds of local churches is an urging of practical considerations and the provision of imaginative models. A theology of mission would take us beyond that modest hope into a consideration of the mission of the church to the nation and the world, but that cannot be developed on the slender foundation of seeking different kinds of local church. The result is that a useful policy receives a framework that is narrow and misleading. Since the report is now being widely used in the training of people for public ministry, it is important that these limitations are clearly understood.

Postscript

I share the hopes expressed so poignantly in this document for a renewal of the church. I want to see local congregations growing; I share the hope that the received parochial structure will not inhibit the appearance of new expressions of church. I want to see cell churches, café churches, theatre, pub and school churches, network and interest group churches. But the reason I want these is because I want the Church of England to become a prophetic church, a church that refuses to accept the poverty which is still so widespread in our society, that refuses to accept the marginalization of so many disabled people, a church that accepts and promotes the equal ministry of men and women, seeks to eliminate from its language the long shadows of oppression, a church that works in dialogue with other great faith traditions in establishing peace and harmony, a church that understands and welcomes diversity, sees the face of Christ in the other, a church that perceives the Spirit of God at work in the world outside the church, a church of the Magnificat (Luke 1.51f), a church that hears the Sermon on the Plain (Luke 6.17–26), a church that not only hears but does the word of God, a church that calls men and women, boys and girls into discipleship of Jesus. Instead, what we have is a lament over the broken territorialism of the Church of England; a church that sees in its mission little more than the creation of more and more churches, one that manifests an inability to perceive the church through the lens of Christian faith, a church that patronizes the poor, that ignores diversity, clings to an imperial past, and which most disturbing of all is innocent. We looked for a mission-shaped church but what we found was a church-shaped mission.

References

Bosch, David J. (1991), *Transforming Mission: Paradigm Shifts in Theology of Mission*, Maryknoll, NY: Orbis Books

Croft, Steven (2002), *Transforming Communities: Re-imagining the Church for the 21st Century*, London: Darton, Longman and Todd

Donovan, Vincent J. (1982), *Christianity Re-discovered: An Epistle from the Masai*, London: SCM Press

Duchrow, Ulrich (1995), *Alternatives to Global Capitalism, drawn from Biblical History designed for Political Action*, Utrecht: International Books

Gorringe, Timothy J. (1994), *Capital and the Kingdom: Theological Ethics and Economic Order*, London: SPCK

Hull, John M. (1999), 'Christian Boundaries, Christian Identities and the Local Church', *International Journal of Practical Theology*, Vol. 1, pp. 1–13

Hull, John M. (2002), 'Understanding Contemporary European Religious Consciousness: An Approach through Geo-politics', *Panorama: International Journal of Comparative Religious Education and Values*, Vol. 14 No. 2, Winter, pp. 123–40

McGavran, Donald A. (1955), *The Bridges of God: A Study in the Strategy of Missions*, London: World Dominion Press

Philip, T. V. (1999), *Edinburgh to Salvador: Twentieth Century Ecumenical Missiology, A Historical Study of the Ecumenical Discussions on Missions*, Delhi: Indian Society for Promoting Christian Knowledge

Scherer, James A. and Bevans, Stephen B., eds (1999), *Faith and Culture*, New Directions in Mission and Evangelism series, No. 3, Maryknoll, NY: Orbis Books

Mission-shaped Church: Church Planting and Fresh Expressions of Church in a Changing Context (2004), London: Church House Publishing

Warren, Robert (2004), *The Healthy Churches' Handbook: A Process for Revitalising Your Church*, London: Church House Publishing

World Council of Churches (1964), *The Missionary Structure of the Congregation*, Geneva: WCC

Also by John M. Hull

Sense and Nonsense About God, 1974, SCM Press.

Hellenistic Magic and the Synoptic Tradition, 1974, SCM Press.

School Worship - An Obituary, 1975, SCM Press.

Studies in Religion and Education, 1984, Falmer Press.

What Prevents Christian Adults from Learning? 1985, SCM Press.

The Act Unpacked: The Meaning of the 1988 Education Reform Act for Religious Education, 1989, Christian Education Movement.

Touching the Rock: An Experience of Blindness, 1990, SPCK.

God-Talk with Young Children, 1991, Christian Education Movement.

Mishmash: Religious Education in Multi-Cultural Britain, A Study in Metaphor, 1991, Christian Education Movement.

On Sight and Insight: A Journey into the World of Blindness, 1997, One World Publishers.

Utopian Whispers: Moral, Religious and Spiritual Values in Schools, 1998, RMEP.

In the Beginning There was Darkness: A Blind Person's Conversations With the Bible, 2001, SCM Press.